S0-ALK-705

For Bill, to whom I am devoted. —NRM

For James, who endured my frustration (and many strange meals) with patience and encouragement. For Nancy, for believing I could. To my Heavenly Father, I give all the glory and praise. —MPM

The authors express appreciation to Denise Vitola, JoAnne Horn Burks, and Gwen Choate, who blessed us with their expertise and encouragement throughout this project and to others of our writing flock who helped us keep the faith. We are especially grateful to Dan Case, our devoted publisher, who never gave up.

TABLE OF CONTENTS

6

IN THE BEGINNING...

Although they were born a generation apart, Nancy Robinson Masters and Maurice Parsley Mallow are certain becoming writers, friends, and co-authors of this book were all part of God's perfect plan for their lives.

One morning Nancy asked Maurice to join her in penning a book of devotionals to encourage others who want to pursue their desire to write. Tall, brunette Nancy is a licensed pilot and fulltime freelancer, whose writing and publishing career spans more than three decades. Petite, blonde Maurice is a retired elementary school teacher whose writing career focused on the needs of children in her classroom, and on those of all ages she has served for more than six decades in a variety of church ministries.

Maurice's devotionals present the view of the struggling novice. Nancy's present the practical wisdom of the experienced mentor. Together, their collection of 70 spiritual insights provides a wealth of information and inspiration for believers who want to write, and writers who want to believe.

"Anyone will find this book a treasure of warmth, wit, and wisdom worth reading again and again," declares Dusty Richards, two-time Spur Award winner, Western Writers of America.

Why 70?

Luke 10:1 KJV tells us "the Lord appointed other seventy also, and sent them two and two" to testify of His power. Maurice and Nancy think it is possible the Lord paired an older believer with a younger, or a novice with an experienced mentor.

Author Max Lucado says, "In our faith we leave footprints to guide others. None should be left to walk the trail alone." Like retired teacher Maurice Parsley Mallow, you may be starting on the trail to expand your writing horizons. Or you may be many-times published like award-winning author Nancy Robinson Masters. No matter where you are on the writing trail, each of these devotionals will help you discover you do not walk alone.

Resist the urge to read hurriedly! Take time to laugh, cry, and apply the lessons these writers have learned. (Nancy's airplane caricature or Maurice's sprig of parsley cleverly identify the author of each piece.) Do the "Write Now!" prompts as you go—they're quick, easy, and fun strategies to help you to put your own spiritual discoveries into print.

Luke says those the Lord sent out returned from their mission "with joy." Nancy and Maurice pray you will return from traveling with them with joy, and that you will use that joy to produce footprints of faith in words for others to follow.

GO WRITE YOUR WORLD

—you, then, who teach others, do you not teach yourself?

Romans 2:21 NIV

One of the earliest recorded titles in Ancient Egypt was "sesh," meaning "scribe." Among the first written languages are representations of scribes carrying the tools of their craft (pigments, water pot, and pen). A seated scribe holding a papyrus roll was one of the most popular subjects in Ancient Egyptian art.

Professional scribes were paid by the line. The usual rule was to make each line about as long as the average line of a modern printed page. Scribes were exempt from paying taxes on their earnings. This certainly made it an attractive profession in a world where the Pharaoh's tax rate could put you in the 100 percent bracket. Along with tax-exempt income came the benefits of power and authority. When the scribes concluded, "Thus it is written," they were not to be questioned or argued with.

However, there was a dark side to consider before deciding on a career sharpening reeds and mixing ink. Apprentice scribes suffered extremely harsh treatment for making the slightest mistakes. The Old Kingdom word "seba" for "teach" also means "beat!" A man (women were not permitted to even hold a scroll) did not achieve his "degree in scribe" until around the age of 40. Death awaited those who dared pen anything that angered Thoth, Egypt's ibis-headed scribe deity. Without question, one had to be devoted to become a scribe.

Dictionaries define devoted as "feelings or displays of strong affection or attachment, ardent, consecrated, and dedicated." Synonyms include loyal, committed, faithful, and constant. These words aptly describe my relationship with writing for more than three decades.

Tragically, there are still places in our world where writers suffer beatings and death for angering authorities because they are devoted to writing. Each time I pick up a pen or place my fingers on a keyboard, I need to give thanks for those throughout history who paid the price for me to enjoy the freedom and privilege to write. More importantly, I need to give thanks that a devoted God who does not threaten me with beatings or death when I make mistakes was willing to pay the price to put Himself into written words for me.

Author Lisa Jimenez challenges people to "break through hidden fears and self-limiting beliefs to live a more outrageous, faith-filled life." Poet Bliss Carman wrote, "Set me a task in which I can put something of my very self, and it is a task no longer; it is joy; it is art." A handout I received at a conference reads, "Blessed is the man who finds out which way God is moving and gets going in the same direction."

Thus it is written. It is time for me to get moving to help a fellow scribe become devoted to writing!

Lord, this is Your work, not mine. Break through my fears and self-limiting beliefs to make me an outrageous, faith-filled learner while teaching another.

Write Now!

List the qualities you remember about one of your favorite teachers.

YOU WANT ME TO DO WHAT?

Even when I am old and gray, do not forsake me, O God....

Psalm 71:18 NIV

"You want me to do what? At my age? You must be kidding."

That was my end of the telephone conversation when Nancy called to suggest we co-author a devotional book to encourage other believers who want to be writers. Nancy has had many years of professional publishing experience authoring articles, stories, poems, and books. Me? I'm a retired elementary school teacher who has only just begun to write all the stories I planned to pen when no longer a slave to the school bell.

I don't consider myself old, but I'm definitely not young anymore. And it is true that I recently wrote a series of short devotionals for an Internet website—even got paid for writing them!

This is different. If I say yes and sign a contract, it will be an obligation that will require me to physically, mentally, and spiritually stretch myself outside my comfort zone. Is my body, as well as my mind, ready for this challenge? I'm afraid to say yes. I'm even more afraid to say no.

Thank You, Lord, for not putting an age limit on the ambitions of my heart. Give me the physical strength and mental courage that comes from knowing You never have, and never will, forsake me when I seek to serve You.

WRITE NOW!
Make a list of things you have done that you didn't think you would ever do.

BASICS FOR BEGINNERS

I passed on to you right from the first what had been told to me, that Christ died for our sins just as the scriptures said he would, and that he was buried, and that three days afterwards he arose from the grave…

1 Corinthians 15:3-4 TLB

Like Paul counseling the new believers at Corinth, I am flattered when asked to counsel beginning writers. Most are confused about the actual writing process that leads to becoming a published author.

I am also fearful. Providing the information beginners need may take only a moment; however, it can often consume many hours. I am grateful for those who took the time to mentor me. I am also grateful for those who prepared me for the difficulty of balancing my desire to help others against the limits of my time.

Let me pass on to you right from the first what has been told to me: Becoming a published author requires learning the basics of writing correct grammar, punctuation, spelling and continually practicing these basics to acquire the skills editors and publishers can trust. Relying on the basics builds confidence that conquers confusion. It worked for the beginning believers in Corinth, and it will work for beginning writers today.

Father, when we become confused as writers, take us back to the basics as believers.

WRITE NOW!

Compose a list of instructions for doing something that was difficult for you as a child, but is easy now, such as how to tie shoes or how to use the potty. Feel free to laugh as you put into words the steps for acquiring the skills you now use as a matter of routine.

WHISPER OR ROAR?

The word which came to Jeremiah from the Lord, saying, "Thus says the Lord, the God of Israel, Write all the words which I have spoken to you in a book."

Jeremiah 30:1-2 NASB

Wow! Imagine, if you can, how it must have been for Jeremiah to hear God say, "I'll tell you the words, and you can write the book."

It must have been awesome! The Scriptures do not say what kind of voice God spoke with. The important fact is that Jeremiah listened and obeyed.

Does God still speak to writers today? Writers like me?

Yes! He may speak in a whisper to my heart, or through the loud roar of some tremendous force of nature that crashes in my ears. He may speak through the voice of another believer, or through the circumstances of my life. Always He speaks through the voice of the Written Word.

Will I be like Jeremiah—willing to listen and obey?

Lord, open my heart to hear You speak the words I am to write.

WRITE NOW!

Have you heard God speak to your heart? Write the words that best describe the message you heard.

MAKE UP YOUR MIND

So I made up my mind that I would not make another painful visit to you.

2 Corinthians 2:1 NIV

Early in my writing career I joined a writers' group. At that time there was no such thing as Caller ID. Each time my telephone rang on Saturday mornings, I hesitated to answer for fear it might be a certain member of the group who always wanted to complain about the comments, critiques, or rejections she received. Listening to her aggravation was the last thing my struggling muse needed. By the time each call ended, her discouragement had replaced my determination to succeed.

I finally made up my mind to use the Apostle Paul plan when she called. If her comments were negative, I responded with something positive. If she pouted about a past disappointment, I praised the possibilities of the present. The more she complained about those who criticized her, the more I bragged on those who helped me.

Her calls, as well as my dread of them, decreased. She finally realized less time spent complaining provided more time for writing!

Oh Lord, surround me with those who have made up their minds to write!

WRITE NOW!

Jot down the name of an author from whom you would like to receive a phone call. Beside the name, write several questions you would ask this person in the conversation.

WHO IS IN CHARGE?

Put God in charge of your work, then what you've planned will take place.

Proverbs 16:3 MSG

Okay, God, I'm ready to write. Inspire me. Put words in my head so I can pour them onto the paper.

My pencils are all sharpened and are in a neat row on my desk, along with my yellow writing pad. A thesaurus and my Bible are nearby. My kitchen is clean from lunch. Soothing music is playing softly in the background. My calendar has been cleared for the afternoon and evening. I have the house all to myself. I even have a scented candle burning. This writing time has been planned for days and all the preparations are in order.

I pick up one of my pencils, ready to let words flow, but no words come. Have I forgotten something? Looking around my desk, I can't see anything missing. I open my Bible and read the verse of Scripture chosen as my focus for today. Still nothing happens.

The verse says to put God in charge of your work, and then what you've planned will take place. That's the answer! With all of my preparation, I left out what is needed most to succeed as a writer: I left out prayer.

Lord, a writer who plans without prayer will usually produce little more than blank pages. Help me put You in charge of the words on the paper before I ever pick up the pencil to write.

WRITE NOW!

Have you started writing something and never finished it? Start over, only this time pray *before* you begin, instead of waiting until you need help to reach the end.

APPROACHING GOLIATH

As Goliath approached, David ran out
to meet him….

1 Samuel 17:48 TLB

What a perfect picture of how a writer feels when facing a deadline! After the thrill of receiving a writing assignment, the task arises in front of you like Goliath approaching with his army.

I've never met a writer who, when given a deadline by an editor, didn't feel the need to get mundane duties out of the way first. We fiddle while feeling overwhelmed. We stall getting started. We cower behind the rocks of our routine, hoping a last-minute rush of inspiration will make up for our dallying.

Fiddling, stalling, and cowering are gigantic problems. They can result in a missed deadline, one of the most serious mistakes a writer can make. David didn't stop to tidy up his tent or stock his freezer with a dozen casseroles in case company came while he was out battling Goliath. His years of shepherding had taught him there was danger in delay. With the enemy advancing, he grabbed his weapon and started swinging as he ran.

God of David, when I have an assignment, let me grab my words and start writing to defeat the foe of delay.

WRITE NOW!

Wear a pair of running shoes when you write. This will remind you to stop procrastinating and get moving!

FACT OR FICTION?

...What we are in word by letters when absent, such persons we are also in deed when present.

2 Corinthians 10:11 NASB

Were Paul to walk into our home or business or place of worship today, I have no doubt he would be exactly the person in the flesh that he is in the words he penned 2,000 years ago. When I read one of his New Testament letters, it's as if I just opened an e-mail from him!

Although e-mail has made correspondence with someone a matter of seconds instead of days or weeks, I still enjoy receiving a letter in my mailbox. I also enjoy sending letters and cards. Something about touching the paper the sender touched seems to make the words more meaningful, more real.

The words I write in my messages should reflect my true feelings. For example, if I sent a card to someone wishing him or her well, but saw that person in need on the street and ignored him or her, my words written in that card would be meaningless.

One of my secret fears of becoming a published author is that I am going to meet people who have read, or will read, this book. What if I don't come across in person the same as I come across in these devotionals?

Oh Lord! Let me live up to what I put down on paper.

WRITE NOW!

Fiction writers use dialogue to create believable characters. Write the words spoken by five famous fiction characters that immediately identify the character without further description being necessary.

TAKE-OFF FEARS

…Some began to sneer… but some…
believed….

Acts 17:32-34 NASB

I was born February 4, the same month and day (though many years after) legendary aviator Charles Lindbergh. While growing up I watched airplanes take off and land near our West Texas cotton farm. An opportunity to pursue my secret childhood dream of becoming a pilot came shortly before my 30th birthday.

"Why are you learning to fly at your age?" skeptical acquaintances sneered when they observed my struggle to acquire a pilot's license. Others reacted with horror or laughter when I replied, "Because I want to."

Before making my first solo flight, I confessed to my flight instructor that the negative comments were creating fear in my own mind about my abilities.

"Stop listening," he warned. "One of the most important things flying teaches you is not to let those who never made a take-off keep you grounded."

Fear can be a healthy thing. It taught me to respect the laws of aerodynamics, to use critical thinking skills, and to take responsibility for my actions. However, fear that paralyzes your perspective to your possibilities is never healthy, no matter what dream you want to pursue. Don't listen when others sneer at your desire to write. Don't be grounded by fear. Believe that you can write, then take off writing what you believe!

Oh God, thank You for putting Yourself into words for us. Give me the courage to put myself into words for You.

WRITE NOW!

> Compose a letter of resignation to a boss named Fear. Include two reasons you no longer will allow Fear to keep you grounded.

HAND WRITING

Now, in these last sentences, I want to emphasize in the bold scrawls of my personal handwriting the immense importance of what I have written….

Galatians 6:11 MSG

Paul and I have something in common. When I wanted my students to understand an important concept, I would write it in bold print on the blackboard. Paul's bold writing was possibly due to a disease of the eyes. Nevertheless, he insisted on writing messages in his own handwriting.

I believe God has given me important words to share with readers. However, it is a struggle for me to use a computer when creating a rough draft. My first writing is done on a yellow legal pad by my own hand. After scratching out, erasing, and correcting my corrections, I feel comfortable transferring my words to the computer.

Someday I hope to master computer technology and that marvelous word-processing machine. For now, my yellow legal pad and pen are my constant companions. Learning it is okay to begin this way has reduced my fear and given me freedom to boldly go where I've never gone before with God.

God, make my words bold in print as well as bold in content when I write in Your name.

WRITE NOW!

Use a pen to write the following sentence in bold print: **I AM A WRITER.**

KING-SIZE MISTAKES

Even though Elnathan and Delaiah and Gemariah pleaded with the king not to burn the scroll, he would not listen to them.

Jeremiah 36:25 NASB

A clipping from a magazine fell out as I opened a note from a friend. The words of international writer and speaker Dr. Ravi Zacharias leaped from the page before me like a flame tossed with gasoline: "God is able to humble each of us without humiliating us, and to elevate all of us without flattering any of us."

Moments earlier I'd opened an envelope returning an entire book manuscript to me with a blunt letter from the editor saying there were errors throughout that had to be corrected. If not, the publishing contract would be cancelled. I wanted to rip the letter to shreds and toss the envelope and all its contents into the fireplace. How dare that editor question my knowledge!

Elnathan, Delaiah, and Gemariah were listening when Jeremiah read from a scroll God had him write to warn King Jehoiakim of impending disaster. They risked their lives attempting to convince the king not to toss the scroll into the fire. Those men were not successful; Ravi Zacharias was. His words caused me to plunge into the task of correcting my mistakes and re-submitting a manuscript that met the requirements of the contract.

Mistakes remind us we are human. Even the most skilled of Iranian rug weavers include an intentional error, known as the Persian flaw, woven into a carpet. We must learn to be humbled, not humiliated, when our mistakes are discovered and be willing to correct them. As King Jehoiakim learned, failure to listen to those who know what we don't want to hear can be the biggest mistake of all.

God, how comforting to know that all the fires of history can never destroy Your perfect Word.

WRITE NOW!

If you find errors in this book, list them here. They are not intentional; they are human.

READY AND WAITING

If I flew on morning's wings to the far western horizon, you'd find me in a minute—you're already there waiting!

Psalm 139: 9-10 MSG

Have you ever been asked who you would choose to have with you if you were marooned with one person on a remote island? Some might choose a famous movie or television star; others might name a sports hero. I would choose my husband. However, the writer of Psalms assures me there would be three of us on this island because God would be there waiting for us when we arrived.

Some days I am ready to go live where there are no telephones, radios, televisions, or doorbells. Just me and my pen, paper, and a laptop! No distractions, no interruptions. I imagine being there with Him would cause unlimited numbers of words to flow from the rough drafts on my paper into finished prose on my laptop, and then sail through cyberspace to millions of eager readers.

Admittedly, the possibility of this happening to a retired schoolteacher is about as remote as that island is from Brady, Texas. No matter where I am, God is always going to be there with me. He is the unlimited source of my creativity. Never mind the noise and distractions that surround me—surrounding myself with His presence is the secret to achieving my writing goals.

Ever-present God, I claim Your promise that wherever life takes me, You will be there. Impress upon my heart that success is not shutting others out, but letting You in.

WRITE NOW!

Who would you want to have with you and God if you were marooned on a remote island? List nine reasons why.

PLEASE, BE SEATED

Sitting down, Jesus called the Twelve....

Mark 9:35 NIV

Old-time pilots like to brag that they learned to fly by the seat of their pants. This refers to the early days of aviation when airplanes had few reliable instruments. A person learned to fly by listening to the sounds and reacting to the feel of the airplane moving through the air as they sat in the cockpit.

The Scriptures are filled with examples of seat-of-the-pants believers. Zaccheus sat in a tree to see Jesus. A beggar sat by the road to speak to Jesus. Mary, the sister of Martha and Lazarus, sat on the floor to listen to Jesus.

The Lord talked about sitting down to count the cost before beginning a project. Before He fed more than five thousand men, plus an unknown number of women and children, Jesus told the disciples to tell the people to sit down. He often sat before He performed a miracle, broke bread, or spoke words that changed lives.

While a few writers claim to do their best work standing, most authors write by the seat of their pants. They keep their seats in their chairs and don't get up until they finish the job.

Please, be seated!

Lord, keep me sitting down in order to lift You up.

WRITE NOW!

Keep a toy whistle near the chair where you write. Each time you get up to do something that isn't related to what you are working on, blow the whistle on yourself.

PORTION CONTROL

I can do everything through Him who gives me strength.

Philippians 4:13 NIV

What is your favorite verse in the Bible? Philippians 4:13 has been my strength through many situations in my life too numerous to describe. It is the verse the Holy Spirit brings to my mind when I have filled my plate so full there's no room left for the portion God may have planned for me.

Would you believe I decided to join our weekly weight-loss group about the same time I also joined an in-depth Bible study group, which also meets weekly with workbook assignments? These activities were extras added to an already busy schedule of church and civic activities.

Then God served me the opportunity to co-author this book of devotionals.

Oh, my! I will be claiming the strength of this verse often in the weeks ahead.

Lord, fill my cup and empty my plate.

WRITE NOW!

Write a one-word sentence you should use as your reply when you are tempted to take on activities that may fill the time you need to write. Here's a hint: Your sentence should contain the word "no."

DON'T TAKE CHANCES WITH CHOICES

And they drew lots for them, and the lot fell to Matthias; and he was added to the eleven apostles.

Acts 1:26 NASB

Should Simon Peter have held a lot-casting election to choose a man to take the place of Judas Iscariot? Some theologians believe Peter's intentions were good, but his methods were wrong. Others believe Peter got in a hurry, failed to wait for the guidance of the Holy Spirit, and the result was the selection of someone who wasn't the man God had planned to fill the vacancy. No doubt Matthias was an honorable man who met the requirements of an apostle (he had seen the resurrected Lord), yet we never hear another mention of him or his ministry. Almost all scholars agree the disciples simply reverted to their old habits when they drew lots to choose.

The disciples' experience is a reminder to writers not to take chances with choices. Analyze potential markets carefully. Allow the Holy Spirit to guide the writing process. Above all, do not revert to old habits that result in mistakes. Take time to choose wisely what you do with the words you write. They will last for eternity.

I love you, Lord, for choosing me to write for You!

WRITE NOW!

Choose one of your writing habits that you need to change. Write a three-sentence plan of action for making that change happen.

WRITE THERE WITH ME

For God did not give us a spirit of timidity, but a spirit of power....

2 Timothy 1:7 NIV

When I waved goodbye to that last second grade class and went home to retire after 21 years as a teacher, I had a plan in mind: I planned to write books for children. Reading to my students each year had instilled in me a desire to pen my own stories.

When I saw an ad in the local newspaper offering a creative writing course, I eagerly enrolled. I'm not usually timid; however, when I arrived at the door to the classroom the first evening, nagging doubts filled my mind. They threatened to push aside years of inspired intentions. I was about to be the student, not the teacher.

Would the other participants intimidate me? What if some of the others taking this class were my former students? Would there be difficult assignments? Why, oh why, did I enroll in this course?

I took a deep breath, prayed for courage, and turned the doorknob. Something wonderful happened! During the next twelve weeks, I discovered that writing was not so much about my ability, but God's dependability to be "write" there with me.

Lord, thank You for giving me the courage to walk through the doors You open for me.

WRITE NOW!

Describe how you felt the first time you went alone to a place you had never been before.

CONVENIENCE OR COMMITMENT?

But some days later Felix arrived with
Drusilla, his wife….

Acts 24:24 NASB

Secular history tells us Felix was a freed slave who through cruelty and brutality pushed his way into the position of Roman governor in Caesarea. His very name in Greek means "licentious pleasure." The historian Tacitus described him as a man whose life matched his name.

Drusilla was the daughter of Herod Agrippa I. Her father killed the Apostle James. Her great-uncle had John the Baptist beheaded. Her great-grandfather tried to kill Jesus in a decree that resulted in the slaughter of Bethlehem's baby boys.

Talk about a tough audience! How would you like to have Felix and Drusilla in your critique group?

Acts 24:25 TLB says that after hearing God's message of love, forgiveness, and offer of salvation, Felix replied, "...when I have a more convenient time, I'll call for you again." Scripture does not tell us if Felix ever had a more convenient time to accept God's offer.

Writing is not a matter of convenience. It is a matter of commitment. While there will be those like Felix and Drusilla who may refuse to accept the message, God will reward you for being the messenger.

Thank you, Sovereign God, that You already know who will read the words I have not yet written.

WRITE NOW!

Quickly jot down seven things you are committed to do at least once each day. Is writing one of them? If not, mark through one item on your list and replace it with a commitment to write.

FLEDGLINGS NEED FELLOWSHIP

And whether one member suffer, all the members suffer with it; or one member be honoured, all the members rejoice with it.

1 Corinthians 12:26 KJV

I must be the luckiest struggling writer anywhere!

Some time ago I was invited to join a small group of women who write. They come from different towns, from different religious backgrounds, and range in age from who knows to who cares. We e-mail daily. These e-mails may include an inspirational thought, a funny story, or a report of an illness or personal tragedy. They may also include a request asking for help on a writing project, cheers for a member's latest publication success, or tears for one who has received a rejection letter. Some have been published authors for years; others, like me, are just beginning to pursue their calling. All amaze me with their willingness to help each other. When we get together in person, we fellowship as only writers can.

Fledgling writers need support from other writers just as fledgling believers need support from other believers. Being encouraged by these writers is teaching me how to minister to other fledglings who do not have a group of writers with whom they can fellowship.

Lord, I would not be writing this book if it weren't for this fellowship of friends who share my desire to write. Thank You for blessing me with them. May they be blessed by me.

WRITE NOW!

Prepare an ad of no more than 20 words seeking others to form a fellowship of writers in your area.

READY, SET, WAIT!

He said to them, "It is not for you to know times... which the Father has fixed by His own authority.

Acts 1:7 NASB

One of the late cartoonist Charles Schulz's favorite subjects in his *Peanuts* comic strip involves Beagle-dog writer Snoopy waiting for responses from editors at the mailbox. Writers laugh at Snoopy's desperate anticipation, but secretly we identify with his anxiety all too well.

As a child, I was always anxious to get wherever we were going. My dad would not tell me about an upcoming event until the very last minute because he knew I would constantly pester him with, "Is it time yet?" Just as Dad had to remind me I didn't need to keep asking the time because he was watching the clock, Jesus had to remind His disciples that the Father knew exactly what time it was on the Kingdom clock. He didn't want them waiting by the mailbox, so to speak, after He went back to Heaven—He wanted them to be busy doing what He had called them to do until He returned. Praise God, they didn't wait. They got busy writing the Gospels we read today!

The immediacy of Internet technology has not eliminated the mailbox syndrome for writers. We are tempted to sit back and wait like Snoopy for the results after we send a submission. Don't do it. As soon as you submit something, begin writing something new. The Father is watching the clock and there's no time to waste.

Oh Lord, forgive us for wasting time waiting when we need to be writing.

WRITE NOW!

Keep a log for one day of things you did that were a waste of time.

GARAGE SALE

Forget the former things; do not dwell on the past.

Isaiah 43:18 NIV

After an inspection of our closets, cabinets, and storerooms, I discovered many things my husband and I no longer use or need. Cracked picture frames, broken headphones, worn suitcases—it was time we eliminated these things of the past so we could stop stumbling over the pile of clutter.

Each time I begin to write, I need to have a garage sale in my mind. I don't need to carry cracked, broken, and worn mental baggage that hinders my fellowship with Christ into my writing. The clutter of past disappointments can weigh my words down. Holding onto previous mistakes may cause my message to stumble. Focusing on former writing failures will land me flat on my future writing face.

Get rid of the rubbish. Make room for God and He will fill your mind with the new thoughts and sparkling ideas that you need to give your writing a fresh start.

Father, help me not to cling to the broken and worn out baggage of my past that gets in the way of my future.

WRITE NOW!

Compose a list of things you need to get rid of in order to have more room to write.

A GOD WHO CAN MOVE SHADOWS

And Isaiah the prophet cried unto the Lord: And he brought the shadow ten degrees backward, by which it had gone down in the dial of Ahaz.

2 Kings 20:11 KJV

I had waited too long to take off one autumn day. Sunset was about to catch me before I reached my intended destination where I would need to land on an unlighted grass airstrip in the middle of a pasture where cattle grazed.

"Lord, give me just a little more daylight," I prayed as my airplane's propeller whirled me toward the gathering darkness ahead. Suddenly, the last ray of sunlight cut through the shadows, illuminating the runway just off the nose of the airplane. By my calculations that runway should have been another ten minutes ahead. Did God move the runway closer, or did He move the sunset back? Either way, I praised Him for the miracle and promised never again to wait to take off.

Writers always want more time to write. Often it is because we waited too long to start. Before you ask God for more time, make good use of the time you already have.

Forgive me, God, for asking You to move the shadows after I waste the light.

WRITE NOW!

If your boss offered to give you a weekly $50 bonus, or to give you 50 minutes of paid time to write each week, which would you choose? Write your response giving your reasons for the choice you made.

DIVINE APPOINTMENTS

There is an appointed time for everything. And there is a time for every event under heaven—

Ecclesiastes 3:1 NASB

This verse was written just for me. It describes my life to a "T." That's "T" as in time.

I graduated high school at age sixteen, one of the youngest in my class. Much too young for college life, I worked and waited several years to become a student again. Before graduating college, I met and married my husband. We did not have our first child until seven years after we married. Finally returning to finish college, I was old enough to be the mother of most of the freshmen!

The urge to write children's stories became a persistent desire by the time my teaching career ended. Even though it meant going back to the books again, I enrolled in a correspondence writing course. It convinced me my desire to write children's stories came from God.

Since then, writing has brought me successes in several areas. However, I haven't had a children's book published... yet. My life has taught me that God's timing is never a minute too early or a second too late for the events He has appointed for my life. I haven't given up. I've just given God control.

Father, please keep replacing my frustration with faith.

WRITE NOW!

> Complete the following sentence: The best time each day for me to write is...

KEEP CLIMBING

Therefore, ... be steadfast, immovable, always abounding in the work of the Lord, knowing that your toil is not in vain in the Lord.

1 Corinthians 15:58 NASB

We were climbing through a solid overcast. Flying in the clouds requires pilots to trust the airplane's instruments, not their instincts. The instructor sitting beside me in the right seat kept insisting I keep my eyes focused forward scanning the gauges. Turning my head could easily induce vertigo, which would cause me to become disoriented.

Suddenly, something went BANG in the back seat of the Cessna 182! It took every bit of pilot discipline I could muster not to turn my head and look for what had caused the noise.

"Trust the instruments and keep climbing," the instructor calmly repeated.

Later, when we were flying level in clear skies, he told me to turn around and look at what had caused the noise. Potato chips were scattered all over the back seat of the airplane! My wise teacher knew a sack of potato chips would expand and burst at 7,000 feet in an unpressurized airplane. He had placed the sack there to test my ability to handle distractions during stressful circumstances.

Writers can become distracted from their work by things just as insignificant as a sack of potato chips. When things go BANG as you write, focus on the Lord. Trust Him to keep you climbing.

Holy Spirit, it is so comforting to know that You are always beside me, disciplining me to defeat distractions that might detour me from my destination.

WRITE NOW!

Select an item of clothing or jewelry to wear any time you are writing. Tell those around you that when you are wearing this particular hat or pair of earrings you are not to be disturbed unless it is an absolute emergency. Write a description of this item and explain why you chose it as your "do not disturb" sign.

DIVERTICULITIS DISAPPOINTMENT

And we know that in all things God works for the good of those who love Him, who have been called according to His purpose.

Romans 8:28 NIV

The trip had been planned for months. The manuscript I'd worked on for so long was in the mail. The bags were packed, airline tickets purchased, house cleaned, yard trimmed, mail and newspapers discontinued. Then the day before departure, I developed diverticulitis, a miserable inflammation of the colon that caused us to cancel our travel plans.

I was not a happy camper. More than once I questioned God, "Why now, after I've worked so hard to finish writing what You wanted me to write, did this have to happen?"

We don't understand the disappointments in life. However, God assures that if we love Him and are following His will, these things are according to His purpose. His answers are always wiser than our prayers.

God, it is hard to be thankful for diverticulitis! Teach me to see disappointments as evidence of Your loving presence in my life even when the reasons aren't revealed.

WRITE NOW!

Write a brief account of a disappointment that resulted in something good in your life.

FROM COOKING POTS TO CLEAN BOWLS

…And the cooking pots in the Lord's house will be like the bowls before the altar.

Zechariah 14:20 NASB

It was one of the hardest things I'd ever done. I had declined to sign a contract with the new owners of the newspaper where for 23 years I'd been a feature aviation columnist. The contract terms conflicted with my professional convictions.

I dreaded attending my monthly writers' group meeting and considered resigning from the membership. At the last minute I threw a jacket over my shoulders that I'd bought the previous day and went. My dread turned to delight as my fellow writers greeted me with smiles, hugs of encouragement, and laughter. A glance in the restroom mirror after the meeting told me why: A large tag I'd failed to remove hung conspicuously from the shoulder of the jacket. In bold words it proclaimed, "I AM WASHABLE!"

The prophet Zechariah wanted the people who were sad to remember they served a God who could, and would, make all things new. God wanted me to let go of my comfortable old writing pots of columns in order for Him to give me new writing market bowls. Within days of my decision not to sign that contract, new publications began requesting my features. Book publishers bid for my manuscripts. Speaking engagements around the world filled my calendar. Rejoicing replaced remorse as God washed away my concerns. My writing career was not over—it had just taken off!

Heavenly Father, continue washing me with words for the bowls You are preparing for me to fill.

WRITE NOW!

> Keep a mixing bowl and a soft cloth near where you write. Use the cloth to polish the bowl while you organize your thoughts before putting them on paper.

YOU'VE GOT TO BE KIDDING

Be cheerful no matter what; pray all the time; thank God no matter what happens. This is the way God wants you who belong to Christ Jesus to live.

1 Thessalonians 5:16-18 MSG

This is a big order, God. Do You really expect me to live up to this standard?

You ask me to be cheerful when someone has hurt me, or when there is a death in my family or among my friends? You expect me to be cheerful when a writing project I have submitted to an editor is returned with a rejection letter? I am to pray and thank You for whatever happens to me?

Yes. Paul says in his letter to the Thessalonians that this is the way I should live.

I should never, however, try to follow these instructions on my own. God has given me the Holy Spirit, who will lead me through these experiences. All that is needed is to ask for guidance, then follow the Guide! I'm just beginning to understand the phrase, "You have to go through the valleys to appreciate the mountaintops." Rejections can make me a better writer just as difficult times can make me a stronger Christian.

God, thank You that I belong to Christ Jesus, so no matter what happens, it will happen to us together.

WRITE NOW!

Complete the following sentence: No matter what happens, I will thank God for...

PERSISTENCE PAYS

What shall we say then? Shall we continue in sin, that grace may abound?

Romans 6:1 KJV

Persistence is often touted as the secret to becoming a successful writer. We love stories about authors whose manuscripts were rejected many times before becoming bestsellers. These stories encourage us to keep trying, and keep trying we should.

However, to persist in doing what is wrong is foolish. Pharaoh persisted in refusing to let the Children of Israel go from slavery and it cost him his son. Jonah persisted in running from God and it cost him three days in the belly of a fish. Ananias and Saphira persisted in deception and it cost them their lives.

There are writers who persist in doing things wrong, then wonder why they receive rejection wages. They refuse to follow directions. They run from improving their skills. They deceive themselves, believing they can get by with giving less than their best.

Are you determined to be a published writer? Then persist in doing what is right. Otherwise, you may not like the wages your persistence pays.

Stop me, Lord, from persisting in doing what is wrong when I write.

WRITE NOW!

What writing mistake do you find yourself most often repeating? Each day for 21 days, write a warning to yourself to stop persisting in making that mistake.

FORGOTTEN OR FOREVER?

Seest thou a man that is hasty in his words? There is more hope of a fool than of him.

Proverbs 29:20 KJV

Words spoken may be forgotten; words written tend to live on.

My words can influence anyone who reads them. I want them to be a good influence. However, if I write in haste, my words could have a negative effect on readers.

"Think before you write" is posted on my computer table. This little sign warns me of the immense power of words in print to tear down or to lift up.

Remember the little children's chorus, "Oh, be careful little mouth what you say?" I've added another verse: "Oh, be careful big hands what you write."

Holy Spirit, control my hands as they speak words on paper.

WRITE NOW!

Trace the outline of your hands. On each finger write a word or phrase that tells something about your life.

POWER BENEATH THE PAINT

And the Lord answered me, and said, write the vision, and make it plain....

Habakkuk 2:2 KJV

Faded paint. Ragged upholstery. A crack in one of the side windows. Hardly the snazzy airplane I had envisioned to be my classroom for my first flying lesson.

The flight instructor knew exactly what I was thinking as we strolled toward the much-experienced Aeronca Champ trainer. He opened the cowling that covered the airplane's engine and motioned me to look inside. Four new chrome cylinders dazzled my eyes.

"Pretty paint on the outside does not produce the power to climb," he explained. "The engine beneath does."

The prophet Habakkuk was called to write a clear message that would move people to put their trust in God. So are we. Avoid painting your inspirational prose with heavy coats of description, unnecessary adverbs, passive voice sentences, clichés, and repetitious phrases. Begin with plain language and use active verbs to strengthen the message. Most importantly, take time to keep your spiritual engine shining through prayer. It isn't the paint on the outside, but the presence of the Holy Spirit within that produces the power to make your writing soar.

Holy Spirit, polish my heart so that my words will be more than just pretty paint.

WRITE NOW!

Jot down the names of three of your favorite Old Testament people and three of your favorite New Testament people. Beside each name write one or two words that describe ways they served God. For example, Noah built; Paul traveled.

UP BEFORE DOWN

And the Lord said to Samuel, "How
long wilt thou mourn for Saul?"

1 Samuel 16:1 KJV

Four months after retiring from teaching, I broke my ankle. It was a severe break that necessitated a hospital stay followed by weeks with my foot in a cast. While convalescing, I whined to everyone. I mourned that God had changed my retirement plans.

One day a friend came to visit and listened to my complaining for several minutes. Then she stopped me. "The Lord has possibly allowed this accident to happen so you will have more time to look up instead of looking down the road."

Ouch! That hurt! However, it put an end to my pity party. Instead of whining, I began accomplishing things that had been put aside for many months. I had time to write a long letter to missionary friends and read books purchased years ago. There was also more time to research my Bible study guides to learn more about God's Word.

Before retirement I complained about not having time to write. Now, I focus on taking time to look up and praise God first before putting words down.

Master, thank You for turning my whine into more time to shine for You.

WRITE NOW!

List six things you can spend five minutes less time doing each day in order to gain half an hour to write.

CHART THE WRITE COURSE

…And you will be my witnesses in Jerusalem, and in all Judea and Samaria, and to the ends of the earth.

Acts 1:8 NIV

Talk about excited! The National Science Foundation extended an invitation to me to travel as a guest journalist to Antarctica! There was one condition, however, that caused me to think twice before accepting such a fabulous offer: I would have to submit to survival training before going to the South Pole.

Writers seeking to serve the Lord can easily get caught up in the excitement of today's mega-media potential for their work. They dream of their byline appearing on magazines near the grocery store check-out counter, or on the cover of a bestseller that brings an appearance on a major network television show and an around-the-world speaking tour.

There's nothing wrong with lofty goals as long as you arc willing to go through survival training to reach them. Don't ignore small, local, or regional markets—the Jerusalems, Judeas, and Samarias. These will build your readership and hone your skills so that you'll be prepared to avoid the pitfalls along the path to publication.

Almighty Creator, I trust You to chart my course.

WRITE NOW!

You don't have to travel to be a travel writer. Write about the area where you live. Include information you are familiar with that a first-time visitor might find interesting or need to know.

SOAPY SECRETS

But when you pray, go away by yourself, all alone, and shut the door behind you and pray to your Father secretly, and your Father, who knows your secrets, will reward you.

Matthew 6:6 TLB

I'm one of those people who can pray anywhere, anytime—driving down the highway, washing dishes, ironing, or working in my yard. However, my favorite place to pray is in the bathtub when I am alone and the door is closed.

A few of my friends think I'm weird when I tell them the bathtub is where I do some of my best praying. I don't care. Surrounded by the warmth of the water, I cry out loud to God sharing secret burdens for my family, my friends, and my writing dreams. I praise, question, and even argue, while at the same time acknowledging that God knows what is best.

Sometimes God answers my bathtub prayers quickly! I know because while writing these devotionals I needed a Scripture concerning food. Right there in the bathtub I prayed for God to give me the verse to use. A few hours later I discovered not one, but two verses, that were exactly what I needed. During all my years of being a Bible reader, I had never read them before!

Thank you, Father, for the privilege of being able to pray about anything, anytime, anywhere. Even in the bathtub.

WRITE NOW!

Write about your favorite place to pray.

EXCESS BAGGAGE

Now Paul and his companions put out
to sea… but John [Mark] left them
and returned to Jerusalem.

Acts 13:13 NASB

So you promised God a long time ago you would set aside time for writing, but you didn't follow through. Since that time you have been carrying around a suitcase full of guilt that you can't let go. Satan has convinced you that your past neglects have doomed you never to be useable by God again.

Mark became frightened when he saw the dangers and hardships he would encounter traveling with Paul to share the Gospel. Paul branded the young man a failure. God did not! Paul later reveals the tremendous disciple Mark became. We testify to this fact each time we recite the name of the second book of the New Testament!

Ditch the excess baggage of guilt you are dragging around. Clutching Satan's suitcase will keep you from grasping the possibilities God has packed and waiting for you to claim.

Empty my hands, Lord, of the past regrets I am holding on to that are keeping me from reaching for present opportunities to serve You.

WRITE NOW!

Keep an old, soft-sided travel bag near your feet as you write. Each time Satan attempts to use guilt to distract you, give the bag a swift kick.

TOFU TRAGEDY

...We can choose the taste we want in food, and we should choose to follow what is right....

Job 34:3-4 TLB

You would think I was a famous chef by the number of cookbooks in my kitchen. Not so, although I do love to cook. I read cookbooks like others read novels. It isn't surprising to me that cookbooks are one of the largest categories of books published each year.

Just as I have fun experimenting with writing, I have fun experimenting with new recipes and ingredients. Like the time I served guests a new dip that called for tofu as one of the ingredients. Tofu is a soy ingredient, rich in protein. When it is added to a dish, it takes on the flavor of the main ingredient, which in this case was tuna. I followed the recipe directions carefully, but had no previous experience with tofu.

The looks on the faces of my guests when they tasted my tuna-tofu concoction spoke volumes about the disaster my experimenting had created. It was a long time before these friends asked me to bring a dish to any event. If I did, a question always arose with a laugh, "Did you use tofu in this recipe?"

I've had writing failures, too. I followed the writer's guidelines, but the ingredients just didn't mix together to produce a tasty read. My characters, plot, setting, and other elements didn't blend together well, and ended up a tuna-tofu dip of a manuscript that made an editor gag.

Lord, choosing to write is right for me. I'll give up trying recipes that call for tofu, but I won't give up trying to write!

WRITE NOW!

> Write about a cooking failure you've experienced. Add what is needed, or delete what is not needed, to make your article "taste" good when the editor reads it.

ITCHING EARS

…Having itching ears; and they shall turn away their ears from the truth….

2 Timothy 4:3-4 KJV

Have you ever met writers who have itching ears? They ask for critiques, but are not really interested in hearing a truthful response. They're just looking for someone to scratch their egos with glowing accolades. If you won't, they seek someone else who will.

You can't improve your writing skills or your chances of getting published if all you want to hear are compliments. Take the writer's "ear drop" treatment instead. Drop the defensive attitude when someone gives you an honest critique, no matter how painful it may be. While all of us can use a sympathetic scratch at times, we need to listen without turning away. We can then choose to agree, disagree, or disregard the comments.

What if you are the one asked to give a critique? How can you be honest and at the same time helpful? Use the A-B-C method: Always start by complimenting what you liked about the writing. Be specific about things that caused you concern as you read. Be nice, even if you need to be negative. Comments should be kept confidential. Don't discuss your critiques of someone's writing with others unless you have the author's permission. To do so is to violate a privileged trust.

Heavenly Father, when my ears itch, scratch them with the truth.

WRITE NOW!

Use the A-B-C method to critique this book.

MAIL CALL

Therefore encourage one another and
build each other up....

1 Thessalonians 5:11 NIV

I planned. I prepared. I prayed. Nothing happened. No great rush of inspired words poured forth from my heart, mind, or soul. There was a time I would have been discouraged and given up.

Praise the Lord! I have learned there are ways to defeat discouragement! One of my favorite strategies begins with spreading an assortment of greeting cards on my desk. While reading the messages inside each card, God impresses my heart with the name of someone who needs that card.

It takes just a minute to address the envelope, add a personal note to the card, stamp, and seal! An amazing thing happens while I am doing this: I become so encouraged by the words I am sending to others that I want to keep writing long after the last envelope is sealed.

Dear God, what a blessing that You use the words I send to encourage others to return encouragement to me!

WRITE NOW!

Keep a box of greeting cards on hand. When you are discouraged with your writing efforts, select one of the cards, write a note of encouragement beneath the printed message, and mail it to yourself.

DRAW THE LINE

Thou shalt not covet....

Exodus 20:17 KJV

The high-performance biplane rolled to a stop on the ramp next to my dowdy tailwheel trainer. I envied the airshow pilot whose aerobatic skills had made her airplane dance with the sky.

"If I had her airplane, I'd be a better pilot," I grumbled to my flight instructor.

He quietly closed the throttle on my excuse. "When you are a better pilot, you can have an airplane like hers."

Beginning writers, like student pilots, get in a hurry wanting what others have achieved. Plagiarizing what someone else has written—stealing a sentence here, a paragraph there—is a dangerous habit for any writer to fall into. Using another writer's work without asking permission, or giving attribution, is a covetous trap all writers must constantly work to avoid.

It is not wrong to want a spiffy airplane, or to admire another writer's achievements so much you want to emulate them. Just draw a line in your spiritual sand to keep your wants from crossing over into envy territory. Your goal is to grow into the writer God wants you to be, not the writer someone else already is.

As I am preparing to become published, Lord, help me not to steal from those who already are.

WRITE NOW!

Compose a letter to the publisher of this book requesting permission to include several of these devotionals in a book of your own.

SECOND WIND

You were running a good race. Who cut in on you...?

Galatians 5:7 NIV

Oh God, I need my second wind!

I can see the light at the end of this writing assignment tunnel. Things were going so good, but now I can't get motivated to finish the job I committed to do. It seems my storehouse of ideas has been depleted; my faith and confidence are being tested. Like so many beginning writers, I envisioned this being easy, but now I've lost my enthusiasm. I'd rather be in the kitchen baking bread than sitting here in front of a keyboard with an editor's deadline breathing down my neck.

It only takes a small amount of yeast to raise an entire loaf of bread. It only takes a small amount of frustration to flatten my confidence. So much for my devotion to writing. No one is going to read what I write anyway.

Then again, maybe someone will. Maybe Satan is trying hard to cut in on me because he knows God is already preparing a reader for what I write.

Oh God, I need my second wind!

Father, in my weakness I ask for Your strength to finish what Satan wants to stop.

WRITE NOW!

Write the ending of a story, an article, or a poem before you write the beginning.

TRADING PLACES

…The student who has been fully trained will be like the teacher.

Luke 6:40 NCV

"Get the stick back," my grizzled flight instructor growled each time I landed the airplane. It was no use to argue that I did have the control stick all the way back. He had ridden through thousands of student pilot landings in the backseat of the tandem two-seater. He knew the exact position the nose of the airplane needed for the landing to be smooth.

"I give up." Tears of frustration spilled down my cheeks after we thudded to a stop.

"Don't give up," he gently encouraged. "Let's try again, only this time I want you to trade places with me so you can see the correct angle from my point of view."

I grudgingly obeyed. An amazing thing happened when I crawled into the back seat and let the instructor take the controls. After I saw the angle from his point of view, my landings became what he wanted them to be!

Believers sometimes experience what I call "Writer's Thud." No matter how many times we try, the words keep coming out wrong. We plunge ahead, determined to do it our way until we are exhausted from our failures and ready to give up. Don't do it! Get in the back seat and let the Holy Spirit take control of your heart, mind, and soul before you start writing again. Then you will see the correct angle and become the writer He wants you to be.

Train me, Holy Spirit, to write from Your point of view.

WRITE NOW!

When you experience Writer's Thud, take your laptop or pen and paper and write while sitting in the backseat of your car (without the engine running, of course!)

SPRING HAS SPRUNG

The flowers are springing up and the time of the singing of birds has come. Yes, spring is here.

The Song of Solomon 2:12-13 TLB

Spring has truly come to our backyard. Although it is still early, daisies, columbines, snapdragons, and pincushion plants are a profusion of color. My herb bed is coming to life again, as are other plants, flowers, and trees. The birds are singing!

However, when we returned home from a recent trip, we discovered that a late freeze had damaged our five crape myrtle bushes. The tips of their branches had turned dark. These plants have been part of our yard for many years. It will be a waiting game to see if they begin their growing cycle again. What if we have to dig them up and start over again with new plants?

Inspecting those bushes reminded me of one of my writing attempts. After researching, writing, and following the guidelines for submitting, I sent one of my favorite children's stories to a publishing company, confident a sale had been planted. A short time later the manuscript was returned to me with a generic rejection note. I was devastated. No doubt my countenance while reading that note resembled those darkened crape myrtle bushes. I did not understand that writing, submitting, rejection, revising, and submitting again are a natural cycle all writers experience in the process of growing.

The crape myrtle bushes will be replaced. After a time to reflect and make changes to the manuscript, it will be submitted to another publisher, and the waiting game will begin once more. Perhaps this time my manuscript will find a place to bloom!

Lord, You created the cycle of seasons that remind me there are cycles for writers, too. I praise You that for every winter of disappointment, there follows a spring of hope.

WRITE NOW!

Take a pen and notebook to your backyard and list all of the sights, sounds, and smells you experience early in the morning. Go back late in the afternoon and make another list. Use each list to create a different setting for a story using the same characters.

ALL RIGHTS

And you belong to Christ; and Christ belongs to God.

1 Corinthians 3:23 NASB

Knowing your rights as a writer is as important as knowing how to spell and punctuate. A friend called to tell how much he enjoyed reading one of my feature articles in his favorite aviation magazine. He was shocked to learn I had no idea my story had appeared there. I had sold the story to another publication several months earlier. Under the terms of the sales contract and in accordance with the Copyright laws, that publication had purchased "All Rights" to the story. This gave them the right to sell my story to someone else without my knowledge.

Usually I sell "First Rights," which means the publisher may use my article one time, the first time it appears in print. Ownership rights to the article then revert back to me and I can offer the article to other publications for "Reprint Rights." This means other publications may purchase the same article from me to use, knowing it has previously appeared somewhere else.

First rights, Reprint Rights, and All Rights are common terms used in publishing. Think carefully before you agree to sell all rights. If you do, you will no longer have control over that particular article. It will belong totally to the purchaser just as we belong totally to God through Christ when we accept the payment He made for all rights to us on Calvary's cross.

Give God control of your life. The writes will follow!

God, I can never repay the price paid to purchase all rights to me. I gladly release all rights to my words and my life to You.

WRITE NOW!

The Copyright law does not protect an idea. It protects each unique expression of the idea. Use the Biblical account of Daniel in the lion's den to write two different short stories—one from Daniel's viewpoint and one from the viewpoint of the lions. Each of these stories is a unique expression of your idea and is protected by the Copyright laws at the time you create them. This protection is automatic. Filing a Registration of Copyright is not required in order for your stories to be protected by the Copyright laws.

PEACH PECKING

…I am doing a great work and I cannot come down. Why should the work stop while I leave it and come down to you?

Nehemiah 6:3 RSV

A friend wanted me to go shopping and have lunch with her today. She just didn't understand that I needed to stay home and write. I have guilty feelings about telling her no. I feel like a pecked peach!

You've seen a pecked peach. As it begins to ripen on a limb, the birds attack it. When a pecked peach falls to the ground, it quickly rots. We love birds, but we don't want them pecking our peaches. We try to keep the birds away by putting big plastic owls in the trees and hanging belts on the limbs so that when the wind blows, it looks like snakes dangling from the branches. This causes the birds to go somewhere else to peck.

When a couple of folks heard I was writing a book, they started pecking me with negative questions and unsolicited advice. They meant well, each offering suggestions of things they felt would be more profitable for me to spend my time doing. Like Nehemiah, it was necessary for me to tell them that this is a great work God wants me to do. I cannot come down until it is finished.

Lord, tie the plastic owl of persistence around my waist and dangle the belt of determination from my arms so that I may keep producing fruit for You.

WRITE NOW!

Select one of the fruits of the Spirit listed in Galatians 5:22 and use it as the theme of a poem or prayer you write while having lunch alone with the Lord. This would be a good time to practice writing that one-word sentence that includes the word "no."

SOAK BEFORE YOU POUR

For no man can lay a foundation other than the one which is laid, which is Jesus Christ.

1 Corinthians 3:11 NASB

Recently I ran into a man I worked with years ago in the construction business. We met at the building supply store where I was picking up supplies needed to pour the foundation for the house my husband and I were building.

"Whatever you do, be sure you soak the sand with plenty of water before you pour the concrete," the experienced homebuilder cautioned. "If you don't, all of the moisture in the concrete will be absorbed by the sand and your foundation will turn into crumbles."

What does a believer who wants to write need to do to "soak the sand" before pouring concrete; i.e., putting words in print? Does he need to study the markets? Read the writers guidelines? Pray for the Holy Spirit's guidance?

All of the above. There's something else, though. Something Satan hopes you won't do. As you sift through the sands of your plans to become published, you need to honestly answer the question, "What are my true motives for writing?"

Will your answer be like the answers of a group of seminary students who told their professor they signed up for a writing class in order to improve their communication skills for the Lord? Or, will you be as honest as the one student who replied, "I like to sleep late so I took this class because it didn't start until noon."

Master Builder, saturate my heart with such sincere love for You that my words do not become crumbles.

WRITE NOW!

Jesus spent His earthly ministry pouring Himself into his disciples. Pour as many words about yourself as you can write onto a piece of paper in one minute. Then pour as many words about Jesus as you can onto a piece of paper in one minute. Which was easier to do?

WHY AM I WRITING?

Do nothing out of selfish ambition or vain conceit...

Philippians 2:3 NIV

Why am I writing? That's a good question. This dream probably began years ago when I was in elementary school. I wrote short plays, gathered the kids from the neighborhood, and we performed them in our garage. What a shame none of my early "scripts" were saved. I might be a famous playwright by now.

Since childhood I have written other things—travel features, newsletter columns, radio spots—because I have never lost my desire to write. Of course, the thought of my name as the author on the cover of a book is a tremendous boost to my ego. Hearing other authors talk about book signings and autograph parties sounds exciting. Who knows? Fame and fortune could follow, so when it does, I'll try to stay humble when I am around others who want to be writers but aren't published authors like me. They'll wish they could be as successful as I am.

Uh-oh.

"First pride, then the crash—the bigger the ego, the harder the fall." (Proverbs 16:18 MSG) This caution-light verse is a warning! There is nothing wrong with taking pride in my accomplishments, as long as I do not let pride turn my sincere motives into sinful ones.

Dear God, empty me of vain conceit and selfish ambition. Fill me with humility so that what I write honors You more than me.

WRITE NOW!

Following is a list of motives for writing. All are legitimate. Circle the three that you feel most apply to you: to obey God; to praise God; to earn income; to improve my communication skills; to experience personal pleasure; to share my beliefs with others; to express on paper what I cannot express out loud.

If your motives for writing aren't included in the list above, list them here:

WHAT PART OF YET DON'T YOU GET?

I therefore, a prisoner for the Lord, beg you to lead a life worthy of the calling to which you have been called, with all lowliness and meekness, with patience, forbearing one another in love, eager to maintain the unity of the Spirit in the bond of peace.

Ephesians 4:1-3 RSV

It happens to some of the best of writers. Even mature believers. Instead of being eager to maintain the unity of the Spirit when they become published, they flaunt their accomplishment. Lowliness and meekness quickly turn to arrogance toward those who haven't been published... yet.

Ah, that little word "yet." It is a word writers on both sides of the byline need to heed. *Yet* can be used to identify a period of time that has already elapsed. *Yet* can also define a time in the future still to come.

If you become published, be careful not to offend those who aren't. If you haven't been published, don't be offended by someone who has. How should you respond to someone who allows legitimate pride to become haughty vanity and who enjoys reminding you she has achieved something you haven't?

"Yet" her know you appreciate her confirmation of your future success.

Lord, what a blessing to know that You can turn the failures of the past into the promises of the future.

WRITE NOW!

Compose a note of congratulations to a writer who has recently been published. Then compose a note of congratulations to a writer who has not yet been published, expressing your confidence in her future success.

MARK YOUR CALENDAR

Every time you cross my mind, I break
out in exclamations of thanks to God.

Philippians 1:3 MSG

Bobbie battled cancer for several years. Our friendship spanned more than four decades. We were neighbors, played bridge together, and traveled together. These activities with Bobbie have left me with memories to last a lifetime. One of my most special memories of her is how supportive she was of my attempts at writing. She eagerly read every story I wrote.

Bobbie dreamed of going to Hawaii. After she was diagnosed with cancer, her husband promised when she felt like traveling between chemo treatments they would take that trip. Sadly, they never did.

Is there some activity you tell yourself you plan to do in the future? A trip you want to take or a home remodeling project you keep putting off? Perhaps a story you tell yourself you are going to write someday?

Though we may not be battling a terminal illness at this time, all of us, like Bobbie, are running out of somedays.

I've been to Hawaii and it is beautiful. Because she was a believer, Bobbie is in a far more beautiful place today. Someday I am going to write about what a special friend and encourager she was. That someday is today.

Dear God, thank You for giving us friends we enjoy during our earthly days, and for the assurance we have as believers that we will enjoy being together for eternity.

WRITE NOW!

Circle today's date on your calendar. Inside the circle write, "Someday!"

LAST WORDS, OR WORDS THAT LAST?

Jehoram was thirty-two years old when he became king, and he reigned in Jerusalem eight years. He passed away, to no one's regret....

2 Chronicles 21:20 NIV

What's the first thing you read when you open the newspaper? Comics? Sports? Or do you immediately scan the obituary page?

Death has a contract with each of us that none of us can break. Even with the tremendous advances in science, technology, and medicine, a baby born in the United States has a life expectancy of only about 80 years.

Few words in the Scriptures are as sad as Jehoram's obituary. Before you grieve for the King of Judah who passed away to no one's regret, go back to the beginning of Jehoram's life. He carved the words of his own tragic obituary by forsaking the Lord and refusing for eight years to be the faithful leader he had the opportunity to be.

Every life is a pen. What are you writing with yours?

Praise God for Jesus, whose resurrection wrote a new contract guaranteeing life everlasting to all who are willing to sign on the dotted line of faith!

WRITE NOW!

Make sure the last words written about you include words written by you.

THE PROOF IS IN THE PATIENCE

…Be patient with each other, making
allowance for each other's faults….

Ephesians 4:2 NLT

I have a bad habit! I proofread while reading. It matters not what the reading material is—newspapers, magazines, books, and even casual e-mail messages. When there is a misspelled word or incorrect punctuation in someone else's writing, it irritates me. Why didn't the author proofread this? How could he or she have been so careless?

This obsession for perfection distracted my enjoyment of reading until God taught me to control it. He allowed some of my writing to appear with mistakes I had made, and with mistakes that were made in the publication process over which I had no control.

It hurt my ego to learn I make mistakes that I sometimes miss when proofreading. It humbled me to learn that errors can occur in the publication process that reflect on me, even though someone else made them.

It is the same with my life. It is easy to see the mistakes of others while failing to see my own. How it must embarrass Jesus, the Author of my faith, when I make mistakes that reflect on Him.

Oh God, control my impatience with the mistakes of others by reminding me of Your patience when You proofread me.

WRITE NOW!

Copyeditors use specific symbols and markings to indicate mistakes in manuscripts that need correcting. What symbol is used to tell the author to insert a comma? Delete a space? Start a new paragraph? Capitalize a word? If you do not know, consult a stylebook such as *The Little Style Guide to Great Christian Writing and Publishing* by Leonard G. Goss and Carolyn Stanford Goss (Broadman & Holman), or *The Associated Press Style Book*. Several Web sites also list these symbols and markings.

ENDING UP

When they came to the border of Mysia, they tried to enter... but the Spirit of Jesus would not allow them to. So they passed by Mysia and went down to Troas.

Acts 16:7-8 NIV

I looked forward for months to speaking at a women's retreat to be held at a campground near the Guadalupe River. I planned my flight to reach the campground airstrip just before noon. The weather did not cooperate. A line of thunderstorms kept me diverting from my route until I made the decision to turn around and go home. I angrily asked God why He stopped me from getting to that retreat. He answered me through the television meteorologist on the weather channel that evening. A picture flashed across the screen of the retreat campground airstrip. It showed only the tails of submerged airplanes still visible after floodwaters sent the Guadalupe River spilling out of its banks at noon.

In his book, *The Long Dark Night of the Soul*, author Douglas Adams writes: "I may not have gone where I intended to go, but I think I have ended up where I needed to be." The Holy Spirit conceived the idea for this book in my heart several years ago. The journey to get from then to now has certainly not gone the way I intended, but it has ended up where it needed to be.

Years of flying have taught me the course to my destination may not always be a straight line. Years of wrangling with writing have taught me that words can take on a direction of their own with God doing the adding, subtracting, multiplying, and dividing to reach a sum I never could have calculated.

Like the picture flashing across the television screen, the Holy Spirit may quickly reveal the reason that something you wrote did not turn out the way you thought it would. Or, it may take years before you understand. Don't waste time wondering. Keep writing the words, allow the Holy Spirit to guide them, and leave the ending of their journey up to God.

Heavenly Father, I trust You to let my endings become new beginnings.

WRITE NOW!

Use the last sentence of one of the books in the Bible to write the first line of a poem or song of praise.

WEEDING OUT FEAR AND DOUBT

Yes, be bold and strong! Banish fear and doubt! For remember, the Lord your God is with you wherever you go.

Joshua 1:9 TLB

I have a fear of snakes! While working in my yard, I move things around cautiously, especially leaves and rocks. Although I try to be bold and strong, fear and doubt cause me to jump at the slightest rustle when I poke my rake into a flowerbed. I know without clearing out the old leaves and trash, I will never be able to see the future blooms.

After accepting this writing assignment, fear and doubt rustled my thoughts: *Can you really write that many devotionals? When will you find time to do this writing? You aren't an experienced writer. Who do you think you are to tell other people what to do?*

Dwight L. Moody, one of the 20th Century's most courageous speakers, said, "God never made a promise that was too good to be true." When fear and doubt come snaking across my mind, I lean on the same promise God spoke to Joshua to banish them like a gardener leans on her trusty rake.

Divine Protector, give me courage to poke my pencil into the leaves of fear and doubt when they threaten to keep my words from blooming.

WRITE NOW!

Make a list of negative words you need to weed out of your mental vocabulary.

HEART MEDS

…And a time to laugh….

Ecclesiastes 3:4 KJV

I am married to a man 20 years my senior. When we began dating a quarter of a century ago we often discussed how we would deal with situations that resulted from our age difference as we grew older. We agreed that keeping a sense of humor would be one of the best ways to cope with the inevitable challenges.

Last week an insurance agent was helping us fill out forms for additional health care coverage.

"Do you take any daily medications?" the agent asked.

"Oh yes, we read the Bible together every evening," my now hard-of-hearing husband assured.

We shared a huge laugh when my husband realized he had confused "medications" with "meditations."

Vocabulary goofs aren't unusual in manuscripts. Most editors will laugh at an occasional one. However, don't assume it is the editor's job to keep your vocabulary healthy. It is your responsibility to make certain readers see (and hear) the correct word. Using a dictionary, a thesaurus, and other resources available to keep your writing fit is still the best prescription to cure your writing ailments. Learn to laugh at your mistakes, but make sure you take corrective action to avoid a relapse!

Lord, medicate our hearts as we meditate on You.

WRITE NOW!

Taking time for meditation each day is just as important to our spiritual health as taking medications each day for our physical well being. Twice a day write a favorite verse of Scripture on a strip of paper. Collect these verses in an empty pill bottle and pull one out when you are in need of a dose of meditation.

CHEERFUL GIVING

Yes, God will give you much so that you can give away much....

2 Corinthians 9:11 TLB

As a child I often heard the phrase, "Give of your time, talents, and tithe." Long before I knew how to calculate percentages, I knew that a tithe meant one penny out of every dime belonged to God. My parents taught me the joy of giving back to Him what was already His when they gave me tithe money to place in the offering at church.

The Bible says that the Lord loves a cheerful giver. However, I confess that I'm not always cheerful giving away hours and actions to help others.

I've observed the busiest members of our local writers' club give their time to read, critique, and coach people they hardly know. I've watched the most successful members provide programs and teach workshops where beginners like me can glean knowledge that will equip us to compete with them for assignments. They often do it without pay, but always with joy!

My goal is to become like these generous writing club members. I want to learn how to give my time and talent as cheerfully as I gave my tithe when I was a child.

Give me more time and talent as a writer, Lord, so that I can give more to honor You.

WRITE NOW!

Is there a writing contest you would like to enter? Cheerfully encourage another writer to enter it as well.

UNLIMITED PARTNERSHIP

A threefold cord is not quickly broken.

Ecclesiastes 4:12 KJV

When I speak at writing conferences, I frequently meet folks who are teaming up with one another to write a book. They seem a bit surprised when I suggest they test their cooperative work skills by spending some time hoeing weeds together in a cotton field.

My Dad's hoe handle was extra long to match his six-foot-six height. It had a razor sharp blade. He walked the rows of cotton ahead of me, carefully pressing a footprint with his big brogans in the soft, plowed ground for my child-size feet to step in as I followed. My little hoe's blade wasn't very sharp. My eagerness to help often resulted in cotton stalks getting chopped instead of the weeds. My legs had to stop and rest more often than his, but I glowed with pride when Dad told folks I was his partner.

I also glowed with pride when he explained that the two of us were partners with God. Dad taught me that our job was to faithfully hoe the weeds, but it was God who got the glory for producing the crop.

While I have more years of writing experience, Maurice has more years of life experience. Our hoes have different handles. Sometimes my blade wasn't as sharp as hers. We didn't always work at the same pace. However, we were faithful to hoe the words together, and God gets the glory for producing the crop!

Father, thank You for the unlimited possibilities we have with You as our writing Partner.

WRITE NOW!

List the qualities most important to you in a writing partner. Beside this list, write the qualities you believe you have that make you a desirable writing partner.

WELL DONE!

His master replied, "Well done, good and faithful servant…!"

Matthew 25:21 NIV

I was occasionally surprised by impromptu visits to my classroom by the principal. At the conferences following each of these visits, the words I hoped to hear were, "Well done. Keep up the good work."

Most of the time I did. However, there were a few conferences when there were no words of praise or criticism. This was disappointing. Was the principal having a bad day? Or, was it possible I had not put forth my best effort during the evaluation?

Writers who want to become published are encouraged to submit entries to legitimate writing contests. Even if I don't win a prize, I am thrilled when my entry is returned with the comment, "well done," from the judge.

What should I do if there are no words of praise? I can tell myself the judge was having a bad day. Or, I can examine my entry to see if there is a way to improve it before submitting it to another contest. Either way, I must not give up pursuing my calling to write.

Oh Lord, keep reminding me that in order to hear the words, "well done," I must not give up putting forth my best efforts.

WRITE NOW!

Write about an occasion when you were rewarded with the words, "well done."

AN EYE FOR AN I

Because a jealous ear harkens to everything, and discordant grumblings are no secret.

The Book of Wisdom 1:10 NAB

Years ago an editor scribbled across the top of one of my manuscripts, "You have I problems."

Was the editor telling me my vision needed correcting? No. A glance at the numerous pencil marks circling each use of the pronoun *I* put her comment clearly in focus. Repetition of any word is distracting to a reader; repetition of the pronoun *I* is particularly irritating.

Isaiah 14:13-14 KJV reveals the angel Lucifer's envious *I* problem. He arrogantly declares, "I will" five times in two verses! His grumblings made no secret of his intent to "be like the most high," an arrogance that cost him his position in heaven.

Overuse of *I* could cost you sales as a writer. Fewer *I*s for the editor's eyes will give your manuscript more eye-appeal. All in favor of getting rid of too many *I*s, say aye!

Thank you, Most High God, for the editor who diagnosed my I problem.

WRITE NOW!

Circle all the *I* pronouns in this devotional. Could you revise it to eliminate some without changing the message?

MARVELOUSLY MADE

I thank you, High God—You're breathtaking! Body and soul, I am marvelously made! I worship in adoration—what a creation!

Psalm 139:14 MSG

This is one of those Scriptures I read, and then promptly read again because it is so special. To even attempt to understand how God can make me, plus billions of other people, and no two of us be exactly alike is breathtaking! Each of us has a unique personality. Even my thoughts are uniquely my own.

Writers have marvelous opportunities to choose how we use our unique personalities and thoughts. I get to choose whether my words will have a positive or negative impact on readers. I also get to choose to honor or dishonor the High God who created this desire to write within me. While praising God for allowing me to make these choices, I am also overwhelmed by the awesome responsibility that comes with being marvelously made a writer. Do others feel this way?

High God, I worship You with adoration, not only for making me who I am, but also for allowing me to choose to be who You want me to be.

WRITE NOW!

Editors may ask a writer to include a brief credential to appear with an article. Read the following example and then write a credential about yourself to accompany an article about your faith or your desire to be a writer. Remember to always begin your credential with the same name as you use in your byline.

Example: Maurice Parsley Mallow is an active member of her church who regularly contributes articles and interviews to the newsletter.

PAJAMA PRAYERS

…Lord, teach us to pray…

Luke 11:1 KJV

The late James Baldwin, one of the major voices of African-American literature, wrote, "Children have never been very good at listening to their elders, but they have never failed to imitate them."

Four-year-old Mattie reminded me of this when I volunteered to keep her one spring day while her parents worked in their yard.

"Wait," I cautioned as she eagerly stuck her fork into the macaroni and cheese on her lunch plate. "We need to say a prayer first."

Mattie's lower lip began to tremble. "I forgot to bring my pajamas."

I had to laugh. Mattie had learned something many adults haven't. She had been blessed to have parents who taught her to set aside a special time to pray. I also felt the deeper conviction of the Holy Spirit reminding me how careless my prayer life had become.

Too many of us are guilty of using urgent "Lord, help me" spur-of-the-moment prayers as an excuse to avoid setting aside a special time to commune with the Heavenly Father. Offering a cursory acknowledgement to God as you begin chasing the cursor on the computer screen isn't enough. Claim time to be quiet before God and meditate on who He is. Allow Him time to lavish you with the words He longs for you to write.

Lord, teach me to pray when I'm wearing pajamas, and when I'm not.

WRITE NOW!

Write a prayer on paper. After you write your prayer, meditate on the Lord and read His Word for ten minutes. Then write another prayer on paper. Did those ten minutes focused on the Lord and His Word make a difference in your prayers?

PRAY OR PREY?

Keep a cool head. Stay alert. The devil is poised to pounce, and would like nothing better than to catch you napping. Keep your guard up…!

1 Peter 5:8-9 MSG

I first spotted the fluffy white cat one morning from my office window. What a beautiful kitty, I thought, glad for the distraction from the not-so-beautiful rough draft of my column for the church newsletter. Suddenly, the charming cat leaped from the hedge where he had been hiding, and pounced upon an unsuspecting little bird.

My opinion of the big cat changed drastically. He was no longer that magnificent animal I admired; now he was a demon! Oh, no, not a devil dressed in a red cape and carrying a pitchfork, but just as frightening to the helpless bird as that fictitious image artists have often used to depict Satan in art and literature.

Struggling authors beware! Satan is like that charming kitty who lurks about a writer's spiritual neighborhood, ready to pounce.

Keep your guard up. He may be nearby!

Lord, help me pray to avoid becoming prey as I write.

WRITE NOW!

Describe the most frequent distractions Satan uses to thwart you in achieving your writing goals. Describe what action you should take when these distractions occur.

WHO DO YOU RESEMBLE?

…They took note that these men had been with Jesus.

Acts 4:13 NIV

"Do you have a favorite author?"

This is one of the first questions kids ask me during Visiting Author programs.

"Yes. Do you?" I reply.

After the children have had the opportunity to tell me who their favorite author is, I hold up one of my books with my picture on the cover. Sometimes it takes a few moments for them to make the connection that the person in their presence is the same as the person pictured on the cover. What a thrill when one of them blurts out, "Hey! I loved reading that book! You look just like the author!"

Along with the writers of the Scriptures, some of my favorite authors who have influenced me in my Christian journey include Theodore Epp, Bernic May, Fannie Crosby, J. Vernon McGee, Marlene Chase, Max Lucado, and *Peanuts* cartoon character Snoopy! The author who influenced me most, however, was LaDelle Macon Robinson. She never wrote a best-selling book. She never composed a famous hymn. She simply wrote notes of encouragement to me as I pursued my calling to write. Mama closed each note with these words of the philosopher Demetrius written centuries ago: "Everybody reveals his own soul in his letters."

Consider carefully the words you write. They will look just like the author!

Father, may the words I write make me look like You.

WRITE NOW!

Using a pseudonym (false name) is a legitimate technique a writer may employ to disguise her actual identity. Pen a pseudonym you would use if you could not use your real name as an author.

ATTITUDE ADJUSTMENT

Your attitude should be the same as that of Christ Jesus.

Philippians 2:5 NIV

Oh God, I need an attitude adjustment!

Many of my writing friends seem to be successful in their writing endeavors. They have books published and articles in magazines, while my efforts keep falling flat! What's wrong?

Okay, okay, I admit it! Nothing would thrill me more than to have one of my children's stories published with my name as the author. Could it be I long for success in the eyes of my peers rather than in Your eyes?

As a believer, I am aware that I should put Christ first, others second, and myself third. However, my attitude as a struggling writer prevents me from doing so. Help!

God, by admitting my attitude, I am trusting You to adjust it.

WRITE NOW!

Write about a time when God adjusted your attitude.

INVESTMENT STRATEGY

Let the Lord be magnified, which hath pleasure in the prosperity of his servant.

Psalm 35:27 KJV

Prepare now for the attack of the "Prosperity Pickers." The Prosperity Pickers are those who will attack you like a plague of locusts when they learn you (gasp!) accept money for using your talent to write about God.

There have been, still are, and always will be those who write under false faith pretenses. Using the writing talent God gives you to honestly earn income is not the same thing. It is a Biblical method of investment confirmed by the Parable of the Talents in the Gospel of Matthew.

Each of three servants was entrusted with wealth that the Master knew he was capable of handling; each had an equal opportunity to use what he received; and each was required to account for what he did with what he had been given. The first two servants who produced for the Master were rewarded. The third servant who buried his talent, (perhaps the Prosperity Pickers told him to), got nothing except a swift kick out of the estate for being wicked, lazy, and worthless.

Nowhere in this parable does God promise Cadillacs, condos, or cash to the servants. Nowhere does He forbid them to have these things. The servants were not rewarded for their results—they were rewarded for their faithfulness.

Apply that principle and you get a practical investment strategy formula: You (His servant) use the wealth (writing talent) entrusted to you by the Master (God). Your faithfulness brings a reward (earning money as a writer) to you. That equals pleasure for the Lord. Now that's what I call prosperity!

Master, I am humbled to be entrusted with a talent to write. Help me not to bury it, but to use it to produce more for Thee.

WRITE NOW!

Write a brief skit based on the Parable of the Talents set in the present. Be sure to use the term "prosperity pickers" in the title.

MY PLANS, GOD'S DIRECTION

We should make plans—counting on God to direct us.

Proverbs 16:9 TLB

Wouldn't you think that by now I would have learned? I still rush ahead making elaborate plans to take a trip with my husband, to purchase an item, or to begin a new writing project, only to have my plans fail. I start out counting on myself instead of God, then end up tripping over my failures and asking God why

The answer is always the same: I didn't ask God to direct my plans before plunging headlong into them.

When God directs, everything happens at the right time and for the right reasons. His direction always leads to something better than I envision. For example, my desire to quickly have a finished book after I completed my part of this writing assignment did not take into consideration the plan God had for this project. Unknown to me, Nancy was struggling with spiritual issues God knew needed to be resolved. My frustration turned to understanding when she later shared with me some of the reasons things had not gone as quickly as I'd wanted them to go.

Regardless of how long you have been a believer, a writer, or both, God wants to direct your path and plan. Calling on Him before falling over failures is a lesson we never stop learning.

Lord, remind me to be patient during times when You are working with others who are part of Your plan for me.

WRITE NOW!

List three clues that indicate you are driving the wrong direction on a one-way street. List three clues that you may be going the wrong direction on a writing project. Are there any similarities?

APPLY THE ANT PRINCIPLE

What is prayer? Prayer is responding to God, by thought and by deeds, with or without words.

The Book of Common Prayer

Next to rejection, nothing makes a writer cringe as much as being told by an editor to get rid of text. Our words are our babies. We cling to them like a good mother clings to each of her children in a crowded shopping mall. Early in my writing career God blessed me with the opportunity to work with Gwen Choate, a superb writer and editor. Gwen taught me how to apply the "ant principle" of good editing.

"An ant patiently bearing a single grain of food seems insignificant when compared to the wide world around it. Yet, its unselfish performance of duty is important because it serves others in its hill. A single word seems insignificant when compared to the words around it, but if it isn't serving others, it doesn't belong in the hill.

"I may be called on as a writer for what may seem insignificant acts of service for my family, my community, or my church. For example, using my writing skills to record the minutes of our women's meetings at church won't result in my becoming a national best-selling author. However, each tiny grain of service is vital to the ongoing work of God's kingdom."

Lord, how blessed to know those who, as St. Francis of Assisi said, preach the Gospel at all times using words only if necessary.

WRITE NOW!

Listen with a careful ear to the needs of those around you and write them down. As you list each need, ask God to provide someone to meet it. Do not assume you are called to meet all of the needs. You may have done your part by simply compiling the list.

MOSES, MIDIAN, AND ME

Moses answered God, "But why me...?

Exodus 3:11 MSG

I have discovered that I have a lot in common with Moses, the Old Testament hero of faith. When Nancy asked me to leave my comfort zone and move into unfamiliar territory as co-author of this book, I protested. I responded just like Moses when God called him to lead the people of Israel to the Promised Land: "But why me?"

Little did I know how much my life would change when I said yes. My calendar was already filled with things to do, people to see, and places to go. Church meetings, social events, business-related activities with my husband—most had to be put on hold or canceled altogether to accomplish this project.

James will tell you we've had some very "different" meals since I started spending most of my time in my office surrounded by various versions of Scripture and dozens of sticky notes full of scribbles. A few of my friends will tell you I've gone a little wacko with this writing business. Even my cat is ignoring me completely. Deep inside, however, I knew I had to leave my comfort zone just like Moses had to give up Midian if I were to become the writer God wanted me to be. God would not take "no" for an answer from Moses. Neither would He take "no" from me.

Nancy is already talking about writing a second book of devotionals. She is in the process of looking for someone to co-author it with her.

Why not me?

Lord, I praise You and I thank You for leading me out of my comfort zone and into the promises that await me as a writer.

WRITE NOW!

Think about a time in your life when you did not want to take on a new task, but did it anyway. Write a message to Moses sharing your experience.

CLICK TO SAVE

They overcame him [Satan] by the blood of the Lamb and by the word of their testimony....

The Revelation 12:11 NIV

In 1890 Nellie Bly, a young New York reporter whose real name was Elizabeth Cochrane, completed a trip around the world in what was an astounding time of only 72 days, 6 hours, 11 minutes, and 14 seconds. With one finger movement today, an e-mail message can travel around the world via the World Wide Web in less than 14 seconds.

William Cameron Townsend, born six years after Nellie's trip, felt called to minister in Central America. He went there in 1917 with a conviction to share the Gospel with the tribal people of Guatemala. He wasn't having a great deal of success until a leader of the Cakchiquel Indians listened to Townsend read from a Spanish Bible, then asked a simple question that revolutionized Townsend's ministry and the future of Bible translation:

"If your God is so smart, how come He does not write in Cakchiquel?"

Townsend was stunned to discover the Cakchiquel did not speak Spanish! He and his wife spent the next ten years living with the tribe, learning their complex language, creating an alphabet for writing it, and translating the New Testament into it. He founded Wycliffe Bible Translators, an organization that has since become the alphabet maker for more than a thousand tongues.

Cameron Townsend never sent an e-mail—he died in 1982 before this marvelous technology was developed. Yet every time I click "send" with a message that includes a testimony of God's grace, love, mercy, forgiveness, and power, I become a partner with him and with every believer whose writing has shared the Word with the world!

Father, I pray for the spoken languages that still have no written words. Thank You for the technology at my fingertips to click and send the message that saves.

WRITE NOW!

Choose a favorite verse of Scripture and learn to write it in at least three different languages. Could God use you to be an alphabet maker?

LISTEN WHILE YOU WRITE

But even if I am unskilled in speech, yet I am not so in knowledge....

2 Corinthians 11:6 NASB

My father was a bookkeeper by vocation and known as a man of few words. When he did speak, people listened because within his scarcity of words was a wealth of knowledge. Dad was not unskilled in his speech—he simply did not feel comfortable speaking before others. He asked not to be called upon to lead in public prayer at church, yet became a leader of the congregation through other ways of service. One way was being a listener.

Writers must be listeners. The closing phrase of ancient letters penned by scribes, "May you be well when you hear this," implies that scribes not only wrote, but also read communications between two people. According to one source, young scribes were warned: "Take heed how you do your work, for your work is the work of heaven, lest you drop or add a letter of the manuscript when you read it, and so become a destroyer of the world."

The power of today's technology makes it possible for my written words to be heard by more people in one day than all the students who heard me during my teaching career. I need to listen for how my words in print will sound inside another person's head when they are read.

May you be well when you hear this.

Lord, teach me to listen to what I write.

WRITE NOW!

While standing in the middle of the kitchen with the dishwasher filling or the clothes dryer tumbling, read out loud something you have written. Did you hear what you wrote, or did you hear what you *thought* you wrote?

BACK TO TENDING SHEEP

The shepherds returned, glorifying and praising God for all the things they had heard and seen, which were just as they had been told.

Luke 2:20 NIV

It must have been hard for those shepherds to go back to their fields and flocks and resume business as usual after experiencing the very first Christmas. One night you're out in a field under the stars watching sheep when, suddenly, the sky is filled with singing angels announcing the promised Messiah has arrived

Wow! You go, you see, you believe, you rejoice, you tell everyone you meet!

Then it's back to tending the sheep.

Were there those among the shepherds who didn't want to go back? Perhaps they felt they were above doing shepherd duties now that they had been privileged to see Jesus. Perhaps some went back to the fields just to watch the sky and wait for another burst of angelic inspiration.

Beginning writers struggle to succeed. They may finish a manuscript, win a prize in a writing contest, or make a sale to a publisher. Unfortunately, some don't want to go back to "tend the sheep" after these accomplishments. Their egos convince them they no longer need to improve their writing skills. They are content to sit back and wait for another burst of heavenly inspiration to come along.

Becoming a successful writer doesn't work that way. The shepherds had seen the Savior, but they still had an obligation to keep tending their sheep. Writers have an obligation to keep tending their writing no matter how many contests they win or sales they make. Failure to do so is to miss the real blessing of becoming the writer God wants you to be.

Excuse me. I have to get back to tending the sheep.

Good Shepherd, no matter how many successes I may experience, thank You for always leading me to be more than what I am.

WRITE NOW!

Psalm 23 uses several vivid verbs to describe the work of a good shepherd. Write a sentence describing the work of a good writer using one of these verbs. For example, "A good writer *makes* her readers want to keep reading."

IFFIES

Finally, brethren, rejoice, be made complete, be comforted, be like-minded, live in peace....

2 Corinthians 13:11 NASB

The Apostle Paul must have known what it was going to be like for me to co-author a book with one of my best friends. We knew when we began that with two writers involved there would be differences of opinion. We agreed that we each should stand by our individual beliefs and respect the right of the other person to stand by hers.

We rejoiced together when the words worked out just right. We completed our assignments when deadlines loomed. And talk about comforted! We wore each other's shoulder out when sad times came into each of our lives while we were working on these devotionals.

The part about being like-minded was a different story. Our disagreements ranged from rewording a single phrase to revising an entire devotional. God showed us how to resolve these differences by revealing a method that allowed either of us to reject any devotional we were not comfortable with, regardless of who wrote it. We called these pieces of writing our "Iffies."

Satan could have used our Iffies to create dissension and keep us from completing this book. Instead, we sought God's guidance and He gave us a way to assure peace in our partnership.

Lord, I rejoice that You allowed us to accomplish together what neither of us could have accomplished alone.

WRITE NOW!

Never throw an Iffie away. Start a file folder and place any of your writing that you do not feel comfortable with in this file. Go through your file from time to time. You may discover a fresh way to change Iffies into nifty pieces of powerful writing.

STONES WITHOUT WORDS

...I have finished the work you gave me to do.

Ezekiel 9:11 TLB

I spend a lot of time in a cemetery.

No, I am not a funeral director or a preacher. I am the president of Belle Plaine Cemetery Association. The picturesque burial ground atop a hill in Callahan County, Texas, is part of the remains of a once-lively Old West town. I try to attend each funeral service conducted there.

Words carved on the tombstones are fascinating to read. Even more intriguing are the rough-cut rocks scattered throughout Belle Plaine Cemetery with no words inscribed upon them. They mark ancient graves of those buried there long before Callahan County arrived.

Ezekiel Chapter 9 opens with Ezekiel's vision of a man clothed in white linen, who carried a writing kit at his side when summoned by God to the temple altar. The man was given the job of using his writing skills to mark those who were grieved by the rebellion of the people against God. The mark would spare them death. In the last verse of Chapter 9 the man returned to the altar and said, "I have finished the work you gave me to do."

It is comforting to remember that God knows the identities of each person buried at Belle Plaine. The stones without words are a reminder every time I wander this sacred place that I have been called to write. God has given me words and the tools to share them. When I stand before Him, I, too, want to be able to say that I have finished the work He gave me to do.

Omnipotent God, You do not need words carved on stone to know who we are. Thank You for putting Yourself into words so that we can know who You are!

WRITE NOW!

Put on paper now the words you wish to have put on stone later.

BENEDICTION BLESSINGS

The grace of the Lord Jesus Christ, and the love of God, and the fellowship of the Holy Spirit, be with you all.

2 Corinthians 13:14 NASB

When Paul had completed his second letter to the church at Corinth, he closed it with a benediction that contains three of the most powerful words in the vocabulary of a believer who wants to write:

Grace. Love. Fellowship.

It is by Christ's grace I am free to be a writer. It is because God loved me so much that He chose to leave Himself in written words. It is the spirit of fellowship that transpires between a writer and her readers that I long to experience more fully.

Though I may never see their faces or know their names, my heart's desire is that all who read what I write will share with me in the grace, love, and fellowship of the Father, Son, and Holy Spirit.

Amen.

WRITE NOW!

Write.

ABOUT THE AUTHORS

NANCY ROBINSON MASTERS

Nancy Robinson Masters is an award-winning author and inspirational speaker whose writing career began in high school when she volunteered to produce her church's newsletter. She has sold more than 3,000 articles, stories, and poems to magazines, newspapers, and trade journals, including numerous aviation features as a licensed pilot, and while working in the aerospace, agriculture, and petroleum industries. As a freelance writer she has authored books published by Scholastic Children's Press, Franklin Watts, Capstone Press, Masair Publications, and other leading imprints.

Nancy and her husband, Master Pilot Bill Masters, live near Abilene, Texas. When Nancy isn't writing, speaking, or presenting Visiting Author programs in schools across America, she and Bill are active in ministries with their church where Nancy says she does her most important work in life: teaching children in Sunday School. E-mail Nancy at masair@abilene.com and visit her website at http://NancyRobinsonMasters.com.

166

MAURICE PARSLEY MALLOW

Maurice Parsley Mallow is a retired elementary school teacher who serves in a variety of ministries in her church and community. In addition to regularly contributing feature articles to her church newsletter, she has written devotionals for websites and radio broadcasts, serves as Sunday School secretary, is a member of the Church Public Relations Committee, works with the children's programs, and sings in the choir with her husband, James, a retired school band director.

Maurice and James have made their home in Brady, Texas, for more than 40 years. She is a member of Brady's F.M. Richards Memorial Library Board. They have two children: Melodianne, a middle school band director; and Morgan, a nurse. They also have two Miniature Dachshund granddogs, Maggie and Annie. E-mail Maurice at mmallow@classicnet.net and visit her website at http://MauriceParsleyMallow.com.